Live Music!

Strings

Elizabeth Sharma

Wayland

Titles in the series

Brass   Strings
Keyboards   The Voice
Percussion Woodwind

TOPIC CHART	MUSIC		Science	Maths	English	Geography	History	Technology	Art	Religious Education
	Performing and Composing	Knowledge and Understanding								
Chapter 1 What are the strings?	✓	✓	✓		✓		✓	✓		
Chapter 2 Sounding the strings	✓	✓	✓	✓	✓			✓		
Chapter 3 Strings from the past live on!		✓			✓	✓	✓		✓	✓
Chapter 4 Making stringed things	✓	✓	✓		✓			✓	✓	

First published in 1992 by
Wayland (Publishers) Ltd
61 Western Road, Hove
East Sussex BN3 1JD, England

Editor: Cath Senker
Designer: Malcolm Walker
Consultant: Valerie Davies, Primary Adviser,
East Sussex County Council Music School

British Library Cataloguing in Publication Data
Sharma, Elizabeth
   Strings. – (Live Music! series)
   I. Title II. Series
   787

ISBN 0 7502 0407 9

Typeset by Kudos Editorial and Design Services,
Sussex, England
Cover artwork by Malcolm Walker
Printed and bound by Casterman S.A., Belgium

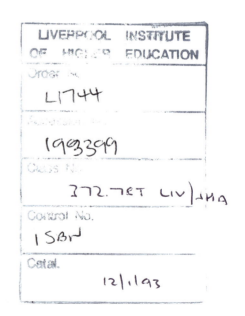

Contents

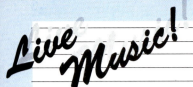

What are stringed instruments?

Have you ever heard a guitar, a violin or a sitar being played? These are all stringed instruments – and there are many more, all around the world.

Stringed instruments come in all shapes and sizes. Some are small and can be held by the player. Others are so big they have to rest on the floor. Some have **frets** to help you play in tune. Stringed instruments can have any number of strings – from one to at least a hundred!

This boy and his father from Nepal are playing typical Nepalese stringed instruments.

In classical style

The **acoustic guitar** is one of the most popular instruments in the world. Here is a classical guitarist. He plays the **melody** or **accompaniment**, exactly as written by the composer.

This is John Williams, a world famous classical guitarist. A classical guitar player usually sits on a chair and rests the right foot on a footstool.

*The acoustic guitar has six strings, **tuned** like this:*

Can you make up a melody on the guitar?

E
A
D
G
B
E

Electric sounds

Guitars are everywhere! Listen to some folk, jazz and rock music. How is the guitar used in each?

You will notice that the electric guitar sounds very different from the acoustic guitar. The electric guitar was invented in 1928. It had to be loud enough to be heard when played with brass and woodwind instruments in large dance halls. In the 1930s big dance bands became very popular in the USA.

*Electric guitars are played in most modern bands. A small microphone is fitted to each guitar, and plugged in to an **amplifier** and speakers.*

The orchestra plays

Look at the youth orchestra below. All the different kinds of instruments are played in an orchestra – strings, woodwind, brass and percussion. The string section is the largest, with up to fifty players.

It is exciting to play in an orchestra. When everyone plays together it is like a wall of different, beautiful sounds around you.

This English youth orchestra is giving an outdoor concert in Germany. The man at the front is the conductor. He directs the orchestra, and makes sure everyone plays at the right time.

The violin family

All the members of the violin family, the violins, violas, cellos and double-basses, are played in the orchestra.

The violin is the smallest of the family. Its strings are tuned to a higher **pitch** than all the other stringed instruments. In an orchestra, the violins usually play the melody.

This Dutch girl is practising the violin. The violin is held under the chin to play.

The viola is a little bigger than the violin. Its strings are tuned to a lower pitch. The viola has a warmer, richer **tone** than the violin. Violas usually accompany the violins in an orchestra, but they hardly ever play the melody.

The cello is a low-pitched instrument. It is too large and heavy to put under your chin, so it rests on the floor. The player sits on a chair and holds the cello between the knees. The cello produces rich, expressive sounds. Listen to a recording of the Dvorak *Cello Concerto* played by Paul Tortelier, and hear how beautiful the cello can sound.

The double-bass is the deepest, lowest-pitched of the string family. It is huge! The player must stand up to play, or sit on a very high stool.

Find a tape of a **symphony orchestra** playing. Or go to hear your local orchestra in concert. You will notice that the string section plays nearly all the time. The strings can play very softly, or very loudly.

Listen for the high pitch of the violins, and the deep, low notes of the cellos and double-basses.

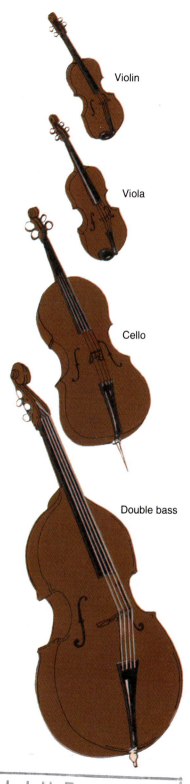

Violin

Viola

Cello

Double bass

Sounding the strings

When you stretch a string across a box and pluck it, the string **vibrates** and makes a musical note. This is the simple idea behind the many kinds of stringed instruments around the world.

Some stringed instruments are plucked, some are played by stroking the strings with a bow, and others are gently struck with little hammers.

A double-bass, with long, thick strings, produces a low sound.

*This Croatian girl is playing the mandolin. She presses two strings together against the **fingerboard.** This shortens the strings, and a higher note is produced. If you turn one of the tuning pegs at the top to make a string tighter, this also makes a higher note.*

A violin has short, thin strings and makes a much higher sound.

Stretch some rubber bands around empty tins or boxes. Use thick and thin rubber bands, and try stretching them by different amounts, so that they are made tighter or looser.

Pluck the bands and listen to the sounds. Press your finger half-way along one of the rubber bands. What happens to the sound?

Sophie, Sharleen and Mario are plucking rubber bands stretched around empty boxes, a coat hanger and some other objects.

Smooth bowing

Many stringed instruments around the world are played with a bow. The bow is made of horse hairs, attached at each end to a thin, curved stick. Using a bow produces longer notes and a smoother sound than plucking the string.

Bowed instruments with several strings must have a high, rounded **bridge** to hold the strings clear of each other. Then you can bow one string at a time.

This man is playing the er-hu, the Chinese violin. The er-hu only has two strings. But he can play many notes on it by changing the length of the strings with his fingers.

The rounded shape of the violin's hollow body and its curved back and front help to produce a clear sound.

Stringed instruments need to have a hollow body to **amplify** the sound of the vibrating string. The f-shaped holes on violins, violas, cellos and double-basses let out the sound. It is like opening your mouth to sing – the sound is much louder than when you hum.

Look at all the stringed instruments in this book and see how the sound is let out in each case.

Strumming along

Guitars can be plucked or **strummed**. You brush all the strings with your fingers to strum. Or you can use a small piece of plastic called a plectrum.

You could learn to strum three simple **chords**.

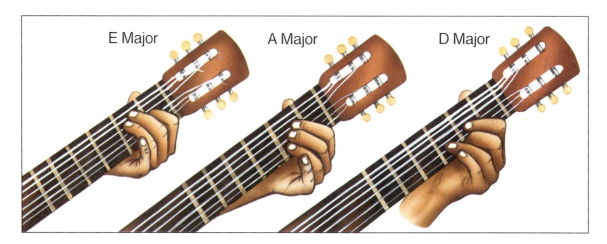

E Major   A Major   D Major

This girl is practising a new chord, F major.

The fingerboard has metal ridges on it, called frets. The frets show you where to place your fingers to play the notes in tune. You can sound good on the guitar even if you can only play a few chords.

The guitar has a round hole to let out the sound, just underneath the place where you strum the strings.

Find out about other instruments that are played like the guitar.

The man on the right is playing a banjo, an instrument originally from Africa. The banjo has frets and is strummed like a guitar. It has a tambourine-like body.

Sweet music

Harps are found all over the world. The player learns to pluck the strings very quickly.

Some stringed instruments have a different string for each note – so there are lots of strings! The strings can be plucked, or struck with small hammers.

This Persian santur (right) is played by striking the strings with small hammers.

Live Music!

When an arrow is released from a bow it makes a twanging sound. It is thought that long ago this gave people the idea of making musical sounds from stretched strings.

The Chinese invented stringed instruments long before the people of Europe. They were playing lutes, lyres and zithers by about 3,000 BC.

Stringed instruments were played in ancient Egypt. This picture was painted on a tomb wall.

We do not know exactly what these ancient instruments sounded like. We can only guess from pictures and writings.

Lutes and lyres are mentioned in the Bible. Can you find out where? If you see paintings of angels, they are often playing harps.

As the centuries passed, it was usual to have musicians at court to entertain the rulers. In many parts of the world, musicians passed on musical skills to their children. It became the tradition for certain families to be music-makers. This still happens in some African countries and in India. Musicians often travelled, taking their instruments to other countries and influencing the music played there.

Music has always been used to celebrate special events. Songs tell of religious and historic happenings. They are usually accompanied by stringed instruments. In this way, stories are passed down through the ages, from the old to the young. Many of these ancient songs and the stringed instruments that were played with them are still with us today.

This viol from the seventeenth century had six strings and frets like a guitar, but was played with a bow. The violin, viola, cello and double-bass developed from viols in the eighteenth century.

The strings of Europe

By the 1500s families of instruments of different sizes were being made in Europe. These included the lute family and the viol family. Well-educated people were expected to be able to sing well, and play instruments in small groups. Music formed an important part of any social event.

This religious painting by a well-known German painter, Grünewald (1455 – 1528), shows an angel playing heavenly music on an instrument similar to a viol.

Gradually, over the next 200 years, the groups playing together grew larger. Stringed instruments were used more than any others in early orchestras. This was partly because early brass and woodwind instruments were rather loud, and not always in tune. Much music has been written for groups of strings. Listen to parts of Vivaldi's *Four Seasons*, composed in the early eighteenth century.

Silken strings from China and Japan

This is a chin, a beautiful, ancient instrument with silk strings. It was in use around 3,000 BC and is still played in China today.

Many Japanese instruments were influenced by the Chinese. The Japanese shamisen is similar in shape to the Chinese er-hu on page 12, but it is plucked, not bowed. The shamisen is played in traditional Japanese theatre to accompany puppet shows and plays.

Balalaikas

Russian balalaikas are made in all different sizes. They are often played in folk orchestras, instead of violins.

You can play the balalaika by strumming the strings with a plectrum. If you strum very fast, you can make long, smooth sounds.

Look at the length of the shamisen's neck! The strings are so long that each one can produce many notes.

This is a small balalaika. The bass balalaika is very large and plays low notes like the cello or double-bass.

Made from a fruit

The kora is an ancient stringed instrument from West Africa. It is made from a large, hard-skinned fruit called a gourd. The gourd is cut in half, hollowed out, and covered with animal skin. The kora player plucks the 21 strings with his thumbs.

Kora players are very much admired and respected. They learn to play from an early age and must be dedicated to their playing.

Sitars and tanpuras

If you have listened to any classical Indian music, then you have probably heard the sitar played. Like the kora, the sitar is made from a gourd. It is decorated with ornate pictures and makes a very special sound.

In Indian music there are many different-sounding **scales**, called ragas. The sitar has strings both above and below the frets.

Ravi Shankar is a famous sitar player, known in the West as well as in India.

There are about 12 strings below the frets, tuned to the raga being used for the melody. They are not plucked, but they vibrate when the other strings above the frets are played, giving an echoing effect.

Above the frets there are seven strings. One is the melody string and the rest are for strumming rhythms. So a sitar player can do three things at once – play the melody, the accompanying raga, and the rhythm.

The tanpura is another Indian instrument. It has four strings that are plucked in turn to make a smooth hum, or **drone**.

Indian musicians remove their shoes as a mark of respect, and sit on the floor. Jermaine is small so he has to kneel to play the tanpura.

Making stringed things

In the 1960s, a kind of folk music called skiffle became popular in Western countries. Groups sang along to acoustic guitars and home-made instruments.

You could make your own double-bass from an upturned bucket. Find a length of thin, nylon fibre string. Tie one end of it to one of the hooks that holds the bucket handle on. Fasten the other end to the top of a broom handle – or use some plastic plumbers' piping.

These young English skiffle players, pictured in 1957, made their own simple double-bass from a tea-chest and a broom handle. People liked skiffle music because anyone could take part.

Sharleen and Sophie are making a plastic bottle harp. Mario is making a bucket bass.

How can you make different notes on your bucket bass? You cannot alter the length by stopping the string with your finger. Work out what to do.

The picture on the right shows an old Egyptian harp. You could make your own harp from a plastic bottle, a cane and some string – see page 27.

Ask an adult to pierce a hole in the top of the bottle. Attach the cane firmly to the other end of the bottle. Cut off three different lengths of string. Tie each string to the cane and through the hole in the end of the bottle.

See what else you can find to make a stringed instrument. Remember, you will always need something to make a hollow body, some sort of neck, and at least one string.

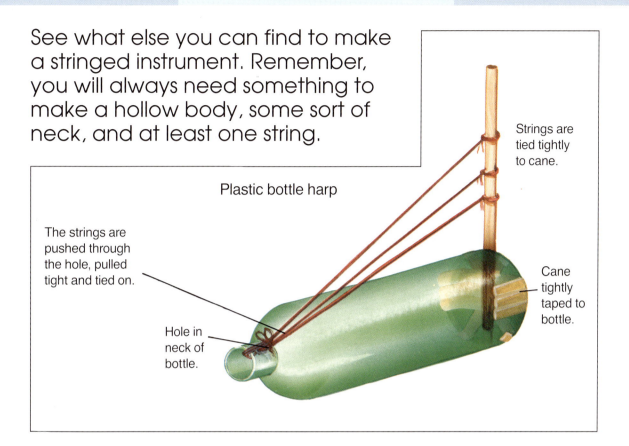

Plastic bottle harp

Strings are tied tightly to cane.

The strings are pushed through the hole, pulled tight and tied on.

Hole in neck of bottle.

Cane tightly taped to bottle.

Concert time!

Here are two ideas for making music to perform in a concert.

1. Practise two easy guitar chords, E major and A minor. These charts show you where to place your fingers:

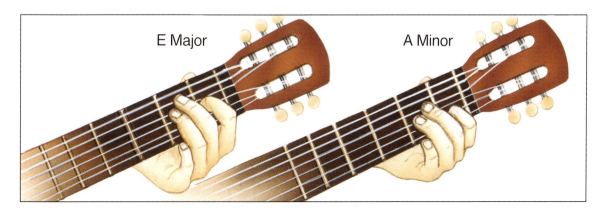

E Major

A Minor

Use these chords to play the spiritual, *Joshua Fought the Battle of Jericho*. The tune could also be played on the violin, recorder or xylophone. Play the bass part on the two lowest strings of a guitar or double-bass, or use your home-made bass.

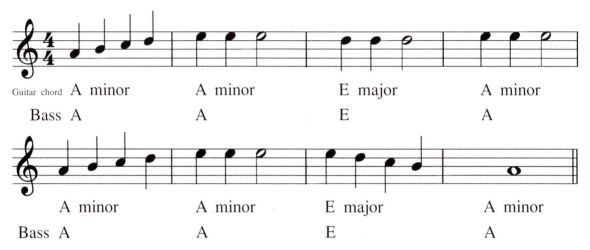

Guitar chord   A minor   A minor   E major   A minor

Bass   A   A   E   A

A minor   A minor   E major   A minor

Bass   A   A   E   A

Two children are playing the tune of Joshua *on the recorder and xylophone. The others are accompanying them on the home-made bucket bass, bottle harp and tambourine.*

2.   Now perhaps you would like to try some Indian music. You can re-tune the lowest three strings of a guitar to play a tanpura drone. Look back to page 24 if you need to remind yourself of what a tanpura is.

Now look back to page 5 to see how to tune a guitar. Tune the lowest E down one note to D. Pluck the three lowest strings over and over again in this pattern (bottom string D, middle string A, top string D'): D D' D' A D D' D' A. This is the drone.

Match the drone to this little tune called *Bamboo Dance*, from north-eastern India. The tune can be played on any instrument, and you can add some parts for your home-made stringed instruments, and percussion.

Glossary

Accompaniment   The part played by an instrument, voices or an orchestra, that accompanies the melody.

Acoustic guitar   A guitar that does not depend on electrical devices to produce a sound.

Amplifier   An electronic device used to make the sound from electric instruments louder.

Amplify   To make louder.

Bridge   A small piece of wood or plastic which holds the strings clear of the fingerboard, and separate from each other.

Chord   A group of notes which are played together to produce an agreeable sound.

Concerto   A piece of music written for a solo instrument accompanied by an orchestra.

Drone   A bass note or chord played over and over again to accompany a melody.

Fingerboard   The part of a stringed instrument against which the strings are pressed to produce different notes.

Frets   Ridges (or arches on the sitar) which mark out the different notes on the fingerboard.

Melody   The correct musical term for a tune.

Pitch   How high or low a note is.

Scales   Groups of musical notes going up or down at fixed intervals.

Strummed   When a group of strings is brushed with the fingers or a plectrum.

Symphony orchestra   A large orchestra with all the instruments needed to play symphonies – strings, brass, woodwind, harp and percussion.

Tone   The quality of a musical sound.

Tuned   Adjusted to a certain pitch.

Vibrates   Shakes rapidly.

Finding out more

1. Why not listen to some string music? Here are some ideas:

Santoor music: *The Best of Shiv Kumar Sharma* and *Music of a Hundred Strings*

Concertos: *Violin Concerto in E minor* by Felix Mendelssohn-Bartholdy
Cello Concerto by Edward Elgar

Orchestral music: *Fantasia on Greensleeves* by Ralph Vaughan Williams

Classical guitar: The slow movement from the *Guitar Concerto* by Joaquin Rodrigo

Harp music: The *Harp Concerto* by Wolfgang Amadeus Mozart

Popular Music: *Bambalayo* by the *Gypsy Kings*

Can you think of at least three words to describe the sounds of each kind of music?

2. Watch concerts on television. There are often programmes showing music from around the world.

3. Try to hear some live music. Most areas have a youth orchestra, and would like to have more people at their concerts. The tickets will be quite cheap. Sometimes musicians from around the world give performances as part of local festivals. Look for posters in your library and ask the librarians.

Useful books

The Eyewitness Guide to Music ed. Janice Lacock (Dorling Kindersley, 1989)
The Guitar by John Bates (Oxford University Press, 1984)
Music by Alan Blackwood (Wayland, 1988)
Music: An Illustrated Encyclopedia by Neil Ardley (Hamlyn, 1986)
Strings by Dee Lillegard (Childrens Press, 1988)

Index

Page numbers in **bold** indicate subjects shown in pictures as well as in the text.

ACKNOWLEDGEMENTS

The photographs in this book were provided by: Bridgeman Art Library 19; J. Allan Cash 7, 10; Cephas (F. Higham) 15; Chapel Studios 14; Eye Ubiquitous 8, (S. Punter) 13; Fotomas Index 18; Michael Holford 17, 26 (below); Horniman Museum 20; Hutchison 22; Photri (A. Kaplan) 16 (above); Rex Features (N. Berman) 6; John Massey Stewart 21; Topham 5, 23, 25; Julia Waterlow 12; Wayland Picture Library (all Garry Fry) *cover*, 11, 24, 26 (above), 28; ZEFA (G. Sirena) 4. Artwork: Creative Hands 5, 14, 20, 21, 27 (both); Malcolm Walker 9. The publishers would like to thank the staff and pupils of the Hammersmith School, London, for their kind co-operation.